Presented to:

Presented by:

Date:

PROMISES FOR MOMENTS OF COMFORT

Reassurement from the Word for a life of acceptance

CHRISTIAN ART PUBLISHERS

Originally published by Honor Books, P O Box 55388, Tulsa, Oklahoma, 74155, under the title *God's Little Book of Promises*

South African edition © 2000
CHRISTIAN ART PUBLISHERS
P O Box 1599, Vereeniging, 1930

First edition 2000

Compiled and edited from the original by Babsie du Toit
Cover designed by Christian Art Publishers

Set in 11 on 13 pt Zurich by Christian Art Publishers

Printed and bound in Singapore

ISBN 1-86852-429-9

00 01 02 03 04 05 06 07 08 09 – 10 9 8 7 6 5 4 3 2 1

Table of Contents

Introduction

God has promised his children many things, including his ever present love, forgiveness and faithfulness. His Word is filled with the promises He has made us. *Promises for moments of comfort* explores God's promises on many issues facing us today.

Whether you are struggling spiritually, looking for a way to encourage a friend, or seeking deeper scriptural understanding, you are sure to find a category or scripture that speaks to your heart. While the world tells us one thing about success, family, temptation, joy, and other issues, the Bible often has some different answers. The topical arrangement of *Promises for moments of comfort* provides quick reference to the truths of God's Word so you can find the truth just when you need it.

God is faithful to his Word and eager to bring it to fullness in our lives. This book is designed to start us on the way and to keep us on the path.

References

The Truth about Joy

For you shall go out in joy and be led forth in peace; the mountains and the hills before you shall break forth into singing, and all the trees of the field shall clap their hands.

Isaiah 55:12 RSV

And the ransomed of the Lord shall return, and come to Zion with singing; everlasting joy shall be upon their heads; they shall obtain joy and gladness, and sorrow and sighing shall flee away.

Isaiah 51:11 RSV

Then he said to them, "Go your way, eat the fat and drink sweet wine and send portions to him for whom nothing is prepared; for this day is holy to our Lord; and do not be grieved, for the joy of the Lord is your strength."

Nehemiah 8:10 RSV

Then will I go to the altar of God, to God, my joy and my delight. I will praise you with the harp, O God, my God.

PSALM 43:4

And provide for those who grieve in Zion – to bestow on them a crown of beauty instead of ashes, the oil of gladness instead of mourning, and a garment of praise instead of a spirit of despair ...

ISAIAH 61:3

I denied myself nothing my eyes desired; I refused my heart no pleasure. My heart took delight in all my work, and this was the reward for all my labor.

ECCLESIASTES 2:10

O Lord, open my lips, and my mouth will declare your praise.

PSALM 51:15

Joy in God

No wonder we are happy in the Lord! For we are trusting him. We trust his holy name.

Psalm 33:21 TLB

I will greatly rejoice in the Lord, my soul shall exult in my God; for he has clothed me with the garments of salvation, he has covered me with the robe of righteousness, as the bridegroom decks himself with the garland, and as a bride adorns herself with her jewels.

Isaiah 61:10 RSV

My soul is feasted as with marrow and fat, and my mouth praises thee with joyful lips, when I think of thee upon my bed, and meditate on thee in the watches of the night.

Psalm 63:5-6 RSV

Joyful People

Yes, the gladness you have given me is far greater than their joys at harvest time as they gaze at their bountiful crops.

Psalm 4:7 TLB

May those who sow in tears reap with shouts of joy! He that goes forth weeping, bearing the seed for sowing, shall come home with shouts of joy, bringing his sheaves with him.

Psalm 126:5-6 RSV

So you have sorrow now, but I will see you again and your hearts will rejoice, and no one will take your joy from you.

John 16:22 RSV

The Truth about Justice

As for the Almighty, we cannot find Him; He is excellent in power, in judgment and abundant justice; He does not oppress.

Job 37:23 NKJV

Arise, O Lord, in thy anger, lift thyself up against the fury of my enemies; awake, O my God, thou hast appointed a judgment.

Psalm 7:6 RSV

To those who by persistence in doing good seek glory, honor and immortality, he will give eternal life.

Romans 2:7

If we confess our sins, he is faithful and just and will forgive us our sins and purify us from all unrighteousness.

1 John 1:9

But let him who glories glory in this, that he understands and knows me, that I am the Lord who practice steadfast love, justice, and righteousness in the earth; for in these things I delight.

JEREMIAH 9:24 RSV

"I will make justice the measuring line and righteousness the plumb line; hail will sweep away your refuge, the lie, and water will overflow your hiding place."

ISAIAH 28:17

Blessed are they who maintain justice, who constantly do what is right.

PSALM 106:3

The days of the blameless are known to the Lord, and their inheritance will endure forever.

PSALM 37:18

God's Justice

He does not crush the weak, or quench the smallest hope; he will end all conflict with his final victory, and his name shall be the hope of all the world.

Matthew 12:20-21 TLB

God presented him as a sacrifice of atonement, through faith in his blood. He did this to demonstrate his justice, because in his forbearance he had left the sins committed beforehand unpunished.

Romans 3:25

The Lord has made himself known, he has executed judgment, the wicked are snared in the work of their own hands.

Psalm 9:16 RSV

Finding Justice

Follow justice and justice alone, so that you may live and possess the land the Lord your God is giving you.
Deuteronomy 16:20

The king's strength also loveth judgment; thou dost establish equity, thou executest judgment and righteousness in Jacob.
Psalm 99:4 KJV

Learn to do well; seek judgment, relieve the oppressed, judge the fatherless, plead for the widow.
Isaiah 1:17 KJV

But let justice roll down like waters, and righteousness like an everflowing stream.
Amos 5:24 RSV

The Truth about Loneliness

Behold, I am with you and will keep you wherever you go, and will bring you back to this land; for I will not leave you until I have done that of which I have spoken to you.

Genesis 28:15 RSV

"I have sewed sackcloth over my skin and buried my brow in the dust. My face is red with weeping, deep shadows ring my eyes ... "

Job 16:15-16

Let him sit alone in silence, for the Lord has laid it on him.

Lamentations 3:28

God sets the lonely in families, he leads forth the prisoners with singing.

Psalm 68:6

All those who know your mercy, Lord, will count on you for help. For you have never yet forsaken those who trust in you.

PSALM 9:10 TLB

I will never, never fail you nor forsake you.

HEBREWS 13:5 TLB

For I eat ashes as my food and mingle my drink with tears because of your great wrath, for you have taken me up and thrown me aside. My days are like the evening shadow; I wither away like grass.

PSALM 102:9-11

Therefore encourage one another and build each other up, just as in fact you are doing.

1 THESSALONIANS 5:11

Turn to me and be gracious to me, for I am lonely and afflicted. The troubles of my heart have multiplied; free me from my anguish.

PSALM 25:16-17

What to Do When You Are Lonely

The eternal God is thy refuge, and underneath are the everlasting arms.
Deuteronomy 33:27 KJV

Who shall separate us from the love of Christ? Shall tribulation, or distress, or persecution, or famine, or nakedness, or peril, or sword? Yet in all these things we are more than conquerors through Him who loved us. For I am persuaded that neither death nor life, nor angels nor principalities nor powers, nor things present nor things to come, nor height nor depth, nor any other created thing, shall be able to separate us from the love of God which is in Christ Jesus our Lord.
Romans 8:35, 37-39 NKJV

Solitude Instead of Loneliness

Be still, and know that I am God; I will be exalted among the nations, I will be exalted in the earth.

Psalm 46:10

We have thought, O God, on Your lovingkindness, in the midst of Your temple.

Psalm 48:9 NKJV

Early in the morning, before the sun is up, I am praying and pointing out how much I trust in you. I stay awake through the night to think about your promises.

Psalm 119:147-148 TLB

You are my hiding place from every storm of life; you even keep me from getting into trouble! You surround me with songs of victory.

Psalm 32:7 TLB

The Truth about Loss

"And God will wipe away every tear from their eyes; there shall be no more death, nor sorrow, nor crying. There shall be no more pain, for the former things have passed away." Then He who sat on the throne said, "Behold, I make all things new."

Revelation 21:4-5 NKJV

As for man, his days are like grass, he flourishes like a flower of the field; the wind blows over it and it is gone, and its place remembers it no more.

Psalm 103:15-16

Weeping may remain for a night, but rejoicing comes in the morning.

Psalm 30:5

He heals the brokenhearted and binds up their wounds.

Psalm 147:3 NKJV

There is a time for everything, and a season for every activity under heaven ... a time to mourn and a time to dance.

ECCLESIASTES 3:1, 4

For the Lord himself will come down from heaven, with a loud command, with the voice of the archangel and with the trumpet call of God, and the dead in Christ will rise first. After that, we who are still alive and are left will be caught up together with them in the clouds to meet the Lord in the air. And so we will be with the Lord forever. Therefore encourage each other with these words.

1 THESSALONIANS 4:16-18

When they saw him from a distance, they could hardly recognize him; they began to weep aloud, and they tore their robes and sprinkled dust on their heads. Then they sat on the ground with him for seven days and seven nights. No one said a word to him, because they saw how great his suffering was.

JOB 2:12-13

Strength for Loss

To all who mourn in Israel he will give: Beauty for ashes; Joy instead of mourning; Praise instead of heaviness. For God has planted them like strong and graceful oaks for his own glory.

Isaiah 61:3 TLB

Blessed are those who mourn, for they will be comforted.

Matthew 5:4

Shout for joy, O heavens; rejoice, O earth; burst into song, O mountains! For the Lord comforts his people and will have compassion on his afflicted ones.

Isaiah 49:13

For as the sufferings of Christ abound in us, so our consolation also abounds through Christ.

2 Corinthians 1:5 NKJV

Comforting Those with Loss

Rejoice with those who rejoice; mourn with those who mourn.

Romans 12:15

I will turn their mourning into gladness; I will give them comfort and joy instead of sorrow.

Jeremiah 31:13

Therefore, as the elect of God, holy and beloved, put on tender mercies, kindness, humility, meekness ...

Colossians 3:12 NKJV

Blessed be the God and Father of our Lord Jesus Christ, the Father of mercies and God of all comfort, who comforts us in all our tribulation, that we may be able to comfort those who are in any trouble, with the comfort with which we ourselves are comforted by God.

2 Corinthians 1:3-4 NKJV

The Truth about Love

And now these three remain: faith, hope and love. But the greatest of these is love.

1 Corinthians 13:13

Work instead at what is right and good, learning to trust him and love others, and to be patient and gentle.

1 Timothy 6:11 TLB

And above all things have fervent love for one another, for "love will cover a multitude of sins."

1 Peter 4:8 NKJV

And above all these put on love, which binds everything together in perfect harmony.

Colossians 3:14 RSV

Love does no harm to its neighbor. Therefore love is the fulfillment of the law.

Romans 13:10

Keep on loving each other as brothers. Do not forget to entertain strangers, for by so doing some people have entertained angels without knowing it.

HEBREWS 13:1-2

"Because of the increase of wickedness, the love of most will grow cold, but he who stands firm to the end will be saved."

MATTHEW 24:12-13

And live a life of love, just as Christ loved us and gave himself up for us as a fragrant offering and sacrifice to God.

EPHESIANS 5:2

"If you obey my commands, you will remain in my love, just as I have obeyed my Father's commands and remain in his love."

JOHN 15:10

Love between God and Man

For God so loved the world that he gave his only Son, that whoever believes in him should not perish but have eternal life.

John 3:16 RSV

And he will love thee, and bless thee, and multiply thee.

Deuteronomy 7:13 KJV

The Lord sets prisoners free, the Lord gives sight to the blind, the Lord lifts up those who are bowed down, the Lord loves the righteous.

Psalm 146:7-8

The Lord your God is with you, he is mighty to save. He will take great delight in you, he will quiet you with his love, he will rejoice over you with singing.

Zephaniah 3:17

Love between People

You shall not take vengeance, nor bear any grudge against the children of your people, but you shall love your neighbor as yourself: I am the Lord.

Leviticus 19:18 NKJV

For the whole Law can be summed up in this one command: "Love others as you love yourself."

Galatians 5:14 TLB

By this all men will know that you are my disciples, if you have love for one another.

John 13:35 RSV

Beloved, let us love one another; for love is of God, and he who loves is born of God and knows God. He who does not love does not know God; for God is love.

1 John 4:7-8 RSV

The Truth about Marriage

And the Lord God said, It is not good that the man should be alone; I will make him an help meet for him.

Genesis 2:18 KJV

Therefore, as God's chosen people, holy and dearly loved, clothe yourselves with compassion, kindness, humility, gentleness and patience. Bear with each other and forgive whatever grievances you may have against one another. Forgive as the Lord forgave you. And over all these virtues put on love, which binds them all together in perfect unity.

Colossians 3:12-14

"A man will leave his father and mother and be united to his wife ... Therefore what God has joined together, let man not separate."

Matthew 19:5-6

He who finds a wife finds a good thing, and obtains favor from the Lord.

PROVERBS 18:22 NKJV

Marriage should be honored by all, and the marriage bed kept pure, for God will judge the adulterer and all the sexually immoral.

HEBREWS 13:4

But since there is so much immorality, each man should have his own wife, and each woman her own husband.

1 CORINTHIANS 7:2

Therefore, rid yourselves of all malice and all deceit, hypocrisy, envy, and slander of every kind. Like newborn babies, crave pure spiritual milk, so that by it you may grow up in your salvation ...

1 PETER 2:1-2

Are you married? Do not seek a divorce. Are you unmarried? Do not look for a wife.

1 CORINTHIANS 7:27

Husband and Wife

Therefore a man leaves his father and his mother and cleaves to his wife, and they become one flesh.

GENESIS 2:24 RSV

You wives, submit yourselves to your husbands, for that is what the Lord has planned for you. And you husbands must be loving and kind to your wives and not bitter against them, nor harsh.

COLOSSIANS 3:18-19 TLB

You husbands must be careful of your wives, being thoughtful of their needs and honoring them ... Remember that you and your wife are partners in receiving God's blessings.

1 PETER 3:7 TLB

Some Marriage Guidelines

Wives, fit in with your husbands' plans; for then if they refuse to listen when you talk to them about the Lord, they will be won by your respectful, pure behavior.

1 Peter 3:1 TLB

For the wife does not rule over her own body, but the husband does; likewise the husband does not rule over his own body, but the wife does.

1 Corinthians 7:4 RSV

The unbelieving husband is consecrated through his wife, and the unbelieving wife is consecrated through her husband.

1 Corinthians 7:14 RSV

The Truth about Mercy

Let us therefore come boldly unto the throne of grace, that we may obtain mercy, and find grace to help in time of need.

Hebrews 4:16 KJV

But you, O Lord, are a compassionate and gracious God, slow to anger, abounding in love and faithfulness. Turn to me and have mercy on me; grant your strength to your servant ...

Psalm 86:15-16

"But now, for a brief moment, the Lord our God has been gracious in leaving us a remnant and giving us a firm place in his sanctuary, and so our God gives light to our eyes and a little relief in our bondage."

Ezra 9:8

But because of his great love for us, God, who is rich in mercy, made us alive with Christ even when we were dead in transgressions – it is by grace you have been saved.

Ephesians 2:4-5

The Lord's curse is on the house of the wicked, but he blesses the home of the righteous. He mocks proud mockers but gives grace to the humble.

Proverbs 3:33-34

I will make all my goodness pass before thee, and I will proclaim the name of the Lord before thee; and will be gracious to whom I will be gracious, and will show mercy on whom I will show mercy.

Exodus 33:19 KJV

Give knowledge of salvation to his people in the forgiveness of their sins, through the tender mercy of our God.

Luke 1:77-78 RSV

God's Mercy

The Lord is gracious, and full of compassion; slow to anger, and of great mercy. The Lord is good to all: and his tender mercies are over all his works.

Psalm 145:8-9 KJV

Who is a God like you, who pardons sin and forgives the transgression of the remnant of his inheritance? You do not stay angry forever but delight to show mercy.

Micah 7:18

Foreigners will come and build your cities. Presidents and kings will send you aid. For though I destroyed you in my anger, I will have mercy on you through my grace.

Isaiah 60:10 TLB

Finding Mercy

For thou, Lord, art good, and ready to forgive; and plenteous in mercy unto all them that call upon thee.
Psalm 86:5 KJV

Yet the Lord still waits for you to come to him, so he can show you his love; he will conquer you to bless you, just as he said. For the Lord is faithful to his promises. Blessed are all those who wait for him to help them.
Isaiah 30:18 TLB

But the lovingkindness of the Lord is from everlasting to everlasting, to those who reverence him; his salvation is to children's children of those who are faithful to his covenant and remember to obey him!
Psalm 103:17-18 TLB

The Truth about Obedience

And Samuel said, Hath the Lord as great delight in burnt offerings and sacrifices, as in obeying the voice of the Lord? Behold, to obey is better than sacrifice, and to hearken than the fat of rams.

1 Samuel 15:22 KJV

Therefore, O Israel, listen closely to each command and be careful to obey it, so that all will go well with you, and so that you will have many children. If you obey these commands you will become a great nation in a glorious land "flowing with milk and honey," even as the God of your fathers promised you.

Deuteronomy 6:3 TLB

If they obey and serve him, they will spend the rest of their days in prosperity ...

Job 36:11

"Be strong and very courageous. Be careful to obey all the law my servant Moses gave you; do not turn from it to the right or to the left, that you may be successful wherever you go. Do not let this Book of the Law depart from your mouth; meditate on it day and night ... "

JOSHUA 1:7-8

Remind the people to be subject to rulers and authorities, to be obedient, to be ready to do whatever is good ...

TITUS 3:1

Follow my example, as I follow the example of Christ.

1 CORINTHIANS 11:1

We demolish arguments and every pretension that sets itself up against the knowledge of God, and we take captive every thought to make it obedient to Christ. And we will be ready to punish every act of disobedience, once your obedience is complete.

2 CORINTHIANS 10:5-6

Obedient Examples

He who has my commandments and keeps them, he it is who loves me; and he who loves me will be loved by my Father, and I will love him and manifest myself to him.

John 14:21 RSV

Because of your obedience, the Lord your God will keep his part of the contract which, in his tender love, he made with your fathers.

Deuteronomy 7:12 TLB

When you obey me you are living in my love, just as I obey my Father and live in his love.

John 15:10 TLB

It was after he had proved himself perfect in this experience that Jesus became the Giver of eternal salvation to all those who obey him.

Hebrews 5:9 TLB

Being Obedient

And this world is fading away, and these evil, forbidden things will go with it, but whoever keeps doing the will of God will live forever.

1 John 2:17 TLB

And how can we be sure that we belong to him? By looking within ourselves: are we really trying to do what he wants us to?

1 John 2:3 TLB

Forget not my law, but let thine heart keep my commandments: For length of days, and long life, and peace, shall they add to thee.

Proverbs 3:1-2 KJV

But, dearly loved friends, if our consciences are clear, we can come to the Lord with perfect assurance and trust, and get whatever we ask for because we are obeying him and doing the things that please him.

1 John 3:21-22 TLB

The Truth about Patience

You need to keep on patiently doing God's will if you want him to do for you all that he has promised.

Hebrews 10:36 TLB

Love is patient, love is kind. It does not envy, it does not boast, it is not proud.

1 Corinthians 13:4

And so after waiting patiently, Abraham received what was promised.

Hebrews 6:15

A hot-tempered man stirs up dissension, but a patient man calms a quarrel.

Proverbs 15:18

For ye have need of patience, that, after ye have done the will of God, ye might receive the promise.

Hebrews 10:36 KJV

Dear brothers, is your life full of difficulties and temptations? Then be happy, for when the way is rough, your patience has a chance to grow. So let it grow, and don't try to squirm out of your problems. For when your patience is finally in full bloom, then you will be ready for anything, strong in character, full and complete.

JAMES 1:2-4 TLB

Be joyful in hope, patient in affliction, faithful in prayer.

ROMANS 12:12

A man's wisdom gives him patience; it is to his glory to overlook an offense.

PROVERBS 19:11

The end of a matter is better than its beginning, and patience is better than pride.

ECCLESIASTES 7:8

Godly Patience

But You, O Lord, are a God full of compassion, and gracious, longsuffering and abundant in mercy and truth.

Psalm 86:15 NKJV

The Lord is merciful and gracious, slow to anger, and plenteous in mercy. He will not always chide: neither will he keep his anger for ever.

Psalm 103:8-9 KJV

And he passed in front of Moses, proclaiming, "The Lord, the Lord, the compassionate and gracious God, slow to anger, abounding in love and faithfulness, maintaining love to thousands, and forgiving wickedness, rebellion and sin."

Exodus 34:6

Brotherly Patience

And so, as those who have been chosen of God, holy and beloved, put on a heart of compassion, kindness, humility, gentleness and patience; bearing with one another, and forgiving each other, whoever has a complaint against anyone; just as the Lord forgave you, so also should you.

Colossians 3:12-13 NASB

Be humble and gentle. Be patient with each other, making allowance for each other's faults because of your love.

Ephesians 4:2 TLB

You will be anxious to follow the example of those who receive all that God has promised them because of their strong faith and patience.

Hebrews 6:12 TLB

THE TRUTH ABOUT PERSECUTION

Remember the word that I said to you, "A servant is not greater than his master." If they persecuted Me, they will also persecute you.

JOHN 15:20 NKJV

Blessed are those who have been persecuted for the sake of righteousness, for theirs is the kingdom of heaven. Blessed are you when men cast insults at you, and persecute you, and say all kinds of evil against you falsely, on account of Me.

MATTHEW 5:10 NASB

Not only so, but we also rejoice in our sufferings, because we know that suffering produces perseverance; perseverance, character; and character, hope.

ROMANS 5:3-4

Yes, and those who decide to please Christ Jesus by living godly lives will suffer at the hands of those who hate him.

2 TIMOTHY 3:12 TLB

"You have persevered and have endured hardships for my name, and have not grown weary."

REVELATION 2:3

We are hard pressed on every side, but not crushed; perplexed, but not in despair; persecuted, but not abandoned; struck down, but not destroyed.

2 CORINTHIANS 4:8-9

To this very hour we go hungry and thirsty, we are in rags, we are brutally treated, we are homeless. We work hard with our own hands. When we are cursed, we bless; when we are persecuted, we endure it ...

1 CORINTHIANS 4:11-12

Handling Persecution

But we have this treasure in earthen vessels, that the surpassing greatness of the power may be of God and not from ourselves; we are afflicted in every way, but not crushed; perplexed, but not despairing; persecuted, but not forsaken; struck down, but not destroyed; always carrying about in the body the dying of Jesus, that the life of Jesus also may be manifested in our body.

2 Corinthians 4:7-11 NASB

Who shall separate us from the love of Christ? Shall trouble or hardship or persecution or famine or nakedness or danger or sword? No, in all these things we are more than conquerors through him who loved us.

Romans 8:35, 37

Your Persecutors

I say: Love your enemies! Pray for those who persecute you! In that way you will be acting as true sons of your Father in heaven.

Matthew 5:44 TLB

If someone mistreats you because you are a Christian, don't curse him; pray that God will bless him.

Romans 12:14 TLB

If your enemy is hungry, give him food to eat; and if he is thirsty, give him water to drink; for you will heap burning coals on his head, and the Lord will reward you.

Proverbs 25:21-22 NASB

The Truth about Perseverance

May the Lord direct your hearts into God's love and Christ's perseverance.
2 Thessalonians 3:5

[Love] always protects, always trusts, always hopes, always perseveres.
1 Corinthians 13:7

Consider it pure joy, my brothers, whenever you face trials of many kinds, because you know that the testing of your faith develops perseverance. Perseverance must finish its work so that you may be mature and complete, not lacking anything.
James 1:2-4

You need to persevere so that when you have done the will of God, you will receive what he has promised.
Hebrews 10:36

We also rejoice in our sufferings, because we know that suffering produces perseverance; perseverance, character; and character, hope.

ROMANS 5:3-4

"My grace is sufficient for you, for my power is made perfect in weakness." Therefore I will boast all the more gladly about my weaknesses, so that Christ's power may rest on me.

2 CORINTHIANS 12:9

Never be lacking in zeal, but keep your spiritual fervor, serving the Lord. Be joyful in hope, patient in affliction, faithful in prayer.

ROMANS 12:11-12

Brothers, as an example of patience in the face of suffering, take the prophets who spoke in the name of the Lord. As you know, we consider blessed those who have persevered. You have heard of Job's perseverance and have seen what the Lord finaly brought about. The Lord is full of compassion and mercy.

JAMES 5:10-11

Under Trials

We also glory in tribulations, knowing that tribulation produces perseverance; and perseverance, character; and character, hope. Now hope does not disappoint, because the love of God has been poured out in our hearts by the Holy Spirit who was given to us.

Romans 5:3-5 NKJV

Because you know that the testing of your faith develops perseverance. Perseverance must finish its work so that you may be mature and complete, not lacking anything.

James 1:3-4

But if anyone suffers as a Christian, let him not feel ashamed, but in that name let him glorify God.

1 Peter 4:16 NASB

Benefits of Perseverance

You need to persevere so that when you have done the will of God, you will receive what he has promised.
Hebrews 10:36

Take heed to yourself and to the doctrine. Continue in them, for in doing this you will save both yourself and those who hear you.
1 Timothy 4:16 NKJV

But the seed on good soil stands for those with a noble and good heart, who hear the word, retain it, and by persevering produce a crop.
Luke 8:15

The Truth about Protection

If you make the Most High your dwelling – even the Lord, who is my refuge – then no harm wil befall you, no disaster will come near your tent. For he will command his angels concerning you to guard you in all your ways.

Psalm 91:9-11

My people will live in peaceful dwelling places, in secure homes, in undisturbed places of rest.

Isaiah 32:18

You are my hiding place; you will protect me from trouble and surround me with songs of deliverance.

Psalm 32:7

Look to the Lord and his strength; seek his face always.

Psalm 105:4

No weapon forged against you will prevail, and you will refute every tongue that accuses you. This is the heritage of the servants of the Lord, and this is their vindication from me ...

Isaiah 54:17

In peace I will both lie down and sleep; for thou alone, O Lord, makest me dwell in safety.

Psalm 4:8 RSV

Discretion will protect you, and understanding will guard you.

Proverbs 2:11

Lord, you have assigned me my portion and my cup; you have made my lot secure. The boundary lines have fallen for me in pleasant places; surely I have a delightful inheritance.

Psalm 16:5-6

My soul clings to you; your right hand upholds me.

Psalm 63:8

Divine Protection

Fear not, for I am with you, be not dismayed, for I am your God; I will strengthen you, I will help you, I will uphold you with my victorious right hand.

Isaiah 41:10 RSV

The Lord shall preserve you from all evil; He shall preserve your soul. The Lord shall preserve your going out and your coming in from this time forth, and even forevermore.

Psalm 121:7-8 NKJV

When you pass through the waters, I will be with you; and when you pass through the rivers, they will not sweep over you. When you walk through the fire, you will not be burned; the flames will not set you ablaze.

Isaiah 43:2

Finding Protection

The angel of the Lord encamps around those who fear him, and he delivers them. Taste and see that the Lord is good; blessed is the man who takes refuge in him.

Psalm 34:7-8

The Lord is a strong fortress. The godly run to him and are safe.

Proverbs 18:10 TLB

He does not fear bad news, nor live in dread of what may happen. For he is settled in his mind that Jehovah will take care of him.

Psalm 112:7 TLB

The Truth about Provision

The Lord is my shepherd, I shall not want.

Psalm 23:1 RSV

Remember your word to your servant, for you have given me hope. My comfort in my suffering is this: Your promise preserves my life.

Psalm 119:49-50

"The wild animals honor me, the jackals and the owls, because I provide water in the desert and streams in the wasteland, to give drink to my people, my chosen ... "

Isaiah 43:20

He also says, "In the begining, O Lord, you laid the foundations of the earth, and the heavens are the work of you hands."

Hebrews 1:10

Don't worry about things – food, drink, and clothes. For you already have life and a body – and they are far more important than what to eat and wear.

MATTHEW 6:25 TLB

For your Father knoweth what things ye have need of, before ye ask him.

MATTHEW 6:8 KJV

His divine power hath given unto us all things that pertain unto life and godliness.

2 PETER 1:3 KJV

What causes fights and quarrels among you? Don't they come from your desires that battle within you? You want something but don't get it. You kill and covet, but you cannot have what you want. You quarrel and fight. You do not have, because you do not ask God.

JAMES 4:1-2

He provides food for those who fear him; he remembers his covenant forever.

PSALM 111:5

God's Provision

But my God shall supply all your need according to his riches in glory by Christ Jesus.

Philippians 4:19 KJV

He causes the grass to grow for the cattle, and vegetation for the service of man, that he may bring forth food from the earth.

Psalm 104:14 NKJV

And God is able to make all grace abound to you, so that in all things at all times, having all that you need, you will abound in every good work.

2 Corinthians 9:8

Man's Role

Do not be anxious about anything, but in everything, by prayer and petition, with thanksgiving, present your requests to God. And the peace of God, which transcends all understanding, will guard your hearts and your minds in Christ Jesus.

Philippians 4:6-7

Oh, fear the Lord, you His saints! There is no want to those who fear Him.

Psalm 34:9 NKJV

Trust in the Lord instead. Be kind and good to others; then you will live safely here in the land and prosper, feeding in safety. Be delighted with the Lord. Then he will give you all your heart's desires. Commit everything you do to the Lord. Trust him to help you do it and he will.

Psalm 37:3-5 TLB

The Truth about Reconciliation

Pursue peace with all people, and holiness, without which no one will see the Lord: looking carefully lest anyone fall short of the grace of God; lest any root of bitterness springing up cause trouble, and by this many become defiled.

Hebrews 12:14-15 NKJV

"Leave your gift there in front of the altar. First go and be reconciled to your brother; then come and offer your gift."

Matthew 5:24

We are therefore Christ's ambassadors, as though God were making his appeal through us. We implore you on Christ's behalf: Be reconciled to God.

2 Corinthians 5:20

Blessed are the merciful: for they shall obtain mercy.

MATTHEW 5:7 KJV

Do not be overcome by evil, but overcome evil with good.

ROMANS 12:21

Be kind and compassionate to one another, forgiving each other, just as in Christ God forgave you.

EPHESIANS 4:32

... His purpose was to create in himself one new man out of the two, thus making peace, and in this one body to reconcile both of them to God through the cross, by which he put to death their hostility.

EPHESIANS 2:15-16

For if, when we were God's enemies, we were reconciled to him through the death of his Son, how much more, having been reconiled, shall we be saved through his life!

ROMANS 5:10

When You Are Wronged

The discretion of a man makes him slow to anger, and his glory is to overlook a transgression.

Proverbs 19:11 NKJV

Do not resist an evil person. If someone strikes you on the right cheek, turn to him the other also.

Matthew 5:39

And whenever you stand praying, forgive, if you have anything against any one; so that your Father also who is in heaven may forgive you your trespasses.

Mark 11:25 RSV

Take heed to yourselves: If thy brother trespass against thee, rebuke him; and if he repent, forgive him.

Luke 17:3 KJV

When You Are Wrong

But love your enemies, and do good, and lend, expecting nothing in return; and your reward will be great, and you will be sons of the Most High; for he is kind to the ungrateful and the selfish.

Luke 6:35 RSV

Why do you look at the speck of sawdust in your brother's eye and pay no attention to the plank in your own eye? How can you say to your brother, "Let me take this speck out of your eye," when all the time there is a plank in your own eye? You hypocrite, first take the plank out of your own eye, and then you will see clearly to remove the speck from your brother's eye.

Matthew 7:3-5

The Truth about Rejection

Behold what manner of love the Father has bestowed on us, that we should be called children of God! Therefore the world does not know us, because it did not know Him. Beloved, now we are children of God; and it has not yet been revealed what we shall be, but we know that when He is revealed, we shall be like Him, for we shall see Him as He is.

1 John 3:1-2 NKJV

A man of many companions may come to ruin, but there is a friend who sticks closer than a brother.

Proverbs 18:24

Do not cast me away when I am old; do not forsake me when my strength is gone.

Psalm 71:9

The stone the builders rejected has become the capstone ...

PSALM 118:22

"I took you from the ends of the earth, from its farthest corners I called you. I said, 'You are my servant'; I have chosen you and have not rejected you. So do not fear, for I am with you; do not be dismayed, for I am your God. I will strengthen you and help you; I will uphold you with my righteous right hand."

ISAIAH 41:9-10

"There is a judge for the one who rejects me and does not accept my words; that very word which I spoke will condemn him at the last day. For I did not speak of my own accord, but the Father who sent me commanded me what to say and how to say it."

JOHN 12:48-49

As you come to him, the living Stone – rejected by men but chosen by God and precious to him ...

1 PETER 2:4

When You Feel Rejected

For he chose us in him before the creation of the world to be holy and blameless in his sight. In love he predestined us to be adopted as his sons through Jesus Christ, in accordance with his pleasure and will – to the praise of his glorious grace, which he has freely given us in the One he loves.

Ephesians 1:4-6

For the Lord will not forsake his people; he will not abandon his heritage; for justice will return to the righteous, and all the upright in heart will follow it.

Psalm 94:14-15 RSV

Hope for the Rejected

The poor and needy seek water, but there is none. Their tongues fail for thirst. I, the Lord, will hear them; I, the God of Israel, will not forsake them.

Isaiah 41:17 NKJV

And Jesus said, "Neither do I condemn you; go your way. From now on sin no more."

John 8:11 NASB

He was despised and forsaken of men, a man of sorrows, and acquainted with grief; and like one from whom men hide their face, He was despised, and we did not esteem Him. Surely our griefs He Himself bore, and our sorrows He carried.

Isaiah 53:3-4 NASB

The Truth about Relationships

God, who has called you into fellowship with his Son Jesus Christ our Lord, is faithful.

1 Corinthians 1:9

But if we walk in the light, as he is in the light, we have fellowship with one another, and the blood of Jesus, his Son, purifies us from all sin.

1 John 1:7

And the Scripture was fulfilled which says, "Abraham believed God, and it was accounted to him for righteousness." And he was called the friend of God.

James 2:23 NKJV

"My command is this: Love each other as I have loved you. Greater love has no one than this, that he lay down his life for his friends."

John 15:12-13

Houses and wealth are inherited from parents, but a prudent wife is from the Lord.

PROVERBS 19:14

Don't have anything to do with foolish and stupid arguments, because you know they produce quarrels.

2 TIMOTHY 2:23

An offended brother is more unyielding than a fortified city, and disputes are like the barred gates of a citadel.

PROVERBS 18:19

Let your gentleness be evident to all. The Lord is near.

PHILIPPIANS 4:5

Since we live by the Spirit, let us keep in step with the Spirit. Let us not become conceited, provoking and envying each other.

GALATIANS 5:25-26

As the mountains surround Jerusalem, so the Lord surrounds his people both now and forevermore.

PSALM 125:2

Family Relations

Children, obey your parents in the Lord: for this is right.

Ephesians 6:1 KJV

Only be careful, and watch yourselves closely so that you do not forget the things your eyes have seen or let them slip from your heart as long as you live. Teach them to your children and to their children after them.

Deuteronomy 4:9

Marriage is honorable among all, and the bed undefiled ...

Hebrews 13:4 NKJV

For the wife does not rule over her own body, but the husband does; likewise the husband does not rule over his own body, but the wife does.

1 Corinthians 7:4 RSV

OTHER RELATIONSHIPS

A friend loves at all times.

PROVERBS 17:17

Do not forsake your friend and the friend of your father.

PROVERBS 27:10

Therefore if you bring your gift to the altar, and there remember that your brother has something against you, leave your gift there before the altar, and go your way. First be reconciled to your brother, and then come and offer your gift.

MATTHEW 5:23-24 NKJV

Keep on loving each other as brothers.

HEBREWS 13:1

The Truth about Renewal

And do not be conformed to this world, but be transformed by the renewing of your mind, that you may prove what is that good and acceptable and perfect will of God.

Romans 12:2 NKJV

A new heart I will give you, and a new spirit I will put within you; and I will take out of your flesh the heart of stone and give you a heart of flesh. And I will put my spirit within you, and cause you to walk in my statutes and be careful to observe my ordinances.

Ezekiel 36:26-27 RSV

If we confess our sins, he is faithful and just to forgive us our sins, and to cleanse us from all unrighteousness.

1 John 1:9 KJV

But those who hope in the Lord will renew their strength. They will soar on wings like eagles; they will run and not grow weary, they will walk and not be faint.

Isaiah 40:31

Praise the Lord, O my soul ... who satisfies your desires with good things so that your youth is renewed like the eagle's.

Psalm 103:1, 5

Therefore we do not lose heart. Though outwardly we are wasting away, yet inwardly we are being renewed day by day.

2 Corinthians 4:16

God's Renewal

Create in me a clean heart, O God; and renew a right spirit within me.
Psalm 51:10 KJV

Therefore if any man be in Christ, he is a new creature: old things are passed away; behold, all things are become new.
2 Corinthians 5:17 KJV

I will seek that which was lost, and bring again that which was driven away, and will bind up that which was broken, and will strengthen that which was sick: but I will destroy the fat and the strong; I will feed them with judgment.
Ezekiel 34:16 KJV

Renewed Believers

Be made new in the attitude of your minds; and ... put on the new self, created to be like God in true righteousness and holiness.

Ephesians 4:23-24

Brothers, I do not consider myself yet to have taken hold of it. But one thing I do: Forgetting what is behind and straining toward what is ahead, I press on toward the goal to win the prize for which God has called me heavenward in Christ Jesus.

Philippians 3:13-14

Do not lie to one another, since you have put off the old man with his deeds, and have put on the new man who is renewed in knowledge according to the image of Him who created him.

Colossians 3:9-10 NKJV

The Truth about Restoration

Restore to me the joy of thy salvation, and uphold me with a willing spirit. The sacrifice acceptable to God is a broken spirit; a broken and contrite heart, O God, thou wilt not despise.

Psalm 51:12, 17 RSV

Restore us, O God; make your face shine upon us, that we may be saved.

Psalm 80:3

Turn us back to You, O Lord, and we will be restored; Renew our days as of old.

Lamentations 5:21 NKJV

"But the seed on good soil stands for those with a noble and good heart, who hear the word, retain it, and by persevering produce a crop."

Luke 8:15

Restore to me the joy of your salvation and grant me a willing spirit, to sustain me. Then I will teach transgressors your ways, and sinners will turn back to you.

PSALM 51:12-13

Brothers, if someone is caught in a sin, you who are spiritual should restore him gently. But watch yourself, or you also may be tempted. Carry each other's burdens and in this way you will fulfill the law of Christ.

GALATIANS 6:1-2

"And repentance and forgiveness of sins will be preached in his name to all nations, beginning at Jerusalem."

LUKE 24:47

First to those in Damascus, then to those in Jerusalem and in all Judea, and to the Gentiles also, I preached that they should repent and turn to God and prove their repentance by their deeds.

ACTS 26:20

God's Role

The Lord will restore the splendor of Jacob like the splendor of Israel, though destroyers have laid them waste and have ruined their vines.

NAHUM 2:2

And the God of all grace, who called you to his eternal glory in Christ, after you have suffered a little while, will himself restore you and make you strong, firm and steadfast. To him be the power for ever and ever. Amen.

1 PETER 5:10-11

He restores my soul.

PSALM 23:3 NKJV

Our Role

Repent, and let every one of you be baptized in the name of Jesus Christ for the remission of sins; and you shall receive the gift of the Holy Spirit.

Acts 2:38 NKJV

Cast away from you all your transgressions, whereby ye have transgressed; and make you a new heart and a new spirit.

Ezekiel 18:31 KJV

Repent ye therefore, and be converted, that your sins may be blotted out, when the times of refreshing shall come from the presence of the Lord.

Acts 3:19 KJV

The Truth about Resurrection

Jesus said to her, "I am the resurrection and the life. He who believes in Me, though he may die, he shall live. And whoever lives and believes in Me shall never die."

John 11:25-26 NKJV

In a moment, in the twinkling of an eye, at the last trump: for the trumpet shall sound, and the dead shall be raised incorruptible, and we shall be changed.

1 Corinthians 15:52 KJV

You were also raised up with Him through faith in the working of God, who raised Him from the dead.

Colossians 2:12 NASB

"All men will hate you because of me, but he who stands firm to the end will be saved."

Mark 13:13

But if it is preached that Christ has been raised from the dead, how can some of you say that there is no resurrection of the dead? And if Christ has not been raised, our preaching is useless and so is your faith.

1 Corinthians 15:12, 14

And this water symbolizes baptism that now saves you also – not the removal of dirt from the body but the pledge of a good conscience toward God. It saves you by the resurrection of Jesus Christ ...

1 Peter 3:21

For this very reason, Christ died and returned to life so that he might be the Lord of both the dead and the living.

Romans 14:9

"Therefore let all Israel be assured of this: God has made this Jesus, whom you crucified, both Lord and Christ."

Acts 2:36

Christ's Resurrection

Seeing what was ahead, he spoke of the resurrection of the Christ, that he was not abandoned to the grave, nor did his body see decay. God has raised this Jesus to life, and we are all witnesses of the fact. Exalted to the right hand of God, he has received from the Father the promised Holy Spirit and has poured out what you now see and hear.

Acts 2:31-33

Blessed be the God and Father of our Lord Jesus Christ, who according to His abundant mercy has begotten us again to a living hope through the resurrection of Jesus Christ from the dead, to an inheritance incorruptible and undefiled and that does not fade away, reserved in heaven for you, who are kept by the power of God through faith for salvation ready to be revealed in the last time.

1 Peter 1:3-5 NKJV

Believers' Resurrection

For if we have been united together in the likeness of His death, certainly we also shall be in the likeness of His resurrection.

Romans 6:5 NKJV

As in Adam all die, so in Christ all will be made alive.

1 Corinthians 15:22 NASB

I want to know Christ and the power of his resurrection and the fellowship of sharing in his sufferings, becoming like him in his death, and so, somehow, to attain to the resurrection from the dead.

Philippians 3:10-11

And Jesus said to him, "Assuredly, I say to you, today you will be with Me in Paradise."

Luke 23:43 NKJV

The Truth about Shame

Fear not; you will no longer live in shame. The shame of your youth and the sorrows of widowhood will be remembered no more.

Isaiah 54:4 TLB

Indeed, let no one who waits on You be ashamed; let those be ashamed who deal treacherously without cause.

Psalm 25:3 NKJV

May those who hope in you not be disgraced because of me, O Lord, the Lord Almighty; may those who seek you not be put to shame.

Psalm 69:6

Behold, I lay in Zion a stumbling stone and rock of offense, and whoever believes on Him will not be put to shame.

Romans 9:33 NKJV

The moon will be abashed, the sun ashamed; for the Lord Almighty will reign on Mount Zion and in Jerusalem, and before its elders, gloriously.

Isaiah 24:23

What shall we say, then? Shall we go on sinning so that grace may increase? By no means! We died to sin; how can we live in it any longer?

Romans 6:1-2

After this, Job opened his mouth and cursed the day of his birth. He said: "Why did I not perish at birth, and die as I came from the womb?"

Job 3:1, 2, 11

Hope for Shame

We are able to hold our heads high no matter what happens and know that all is well, for we know how dearly God loves us, and we feel this warm love everywhere within us because God has given us the Holy Spirit to fill our hearts with his love.

Romans 5:5 TLB

Therefore being justified by faith, we have peace with God through our Lord Jesus Christ.

Romans 5:1 KJV

There is therefore now no condemnation for those who are in Christ Jesus.

Romans 8:1 NASB

Not Ashamed

But if anyone suffers as a Christian, let him not feel ashamed, but in that name let him glorify God.

1 Peter 4:16 NASB

For I am not ashamed of the gospel of Christ, for it is the power of God to salvation for everyone who believes, for the Jew ... and also for the Greek.

Romans 1:16 NKJV

So do not be ashamed to testify about our Lord, or ashamed of me his prisoner.

2 Timothy 1:8

Be diligent to present yourself approved to God, a worker who does not need to be ashamed, rightly dividing the word of truth.

2 Timothy 2:15 NKJV

The Truth about Stewardship

"Whoever can be trusted with very little can also be trusted with much, and whoever is dishonest with very little will also be dishonest with much. So if you have not been trustworthy in handling worldly wealth, who will trust you with true riches?"

Luke 16:10-11

"The Lord rewards every man for his righteousness and faithfulness. The Lord delivered you into my hands today, but I would not lay a hand on the Lord's anointed."

1 Samuel 26:23

And the God of all grace, who called you to his eternal glory in Christ, after you have suffered a little while, will himself restore you and make you strong, firm and steadfast.

1 Peter 5:10

You will keep in perfect peace him whose mind is steadfast, because he trusts in you.

ISAIAH 26:3

He who is faithful in what is least is faithful also in much; and he who is unjust in what is least is unjust also in much.

LUKE 16:10 NKJV

Now it is required that those who have been given a trust must prove faithful.

1 CORINTHIANS 4:2

As each one has received a gift, minister it to one another, as good stewards of the manifold grace of God.

1 PETER 4:10 NKJV

Good will come to him who is generous and lends freely, who conducts his affairs with justice.

PSALM 112:5

Since we live by the Spirit, let us keep in step with the Spirit.

GALATIANS 5:25

Godly Stewards

Moreover it is required in stewards that one be found faithful.

1 Corinthians 4:2 NKJV

And he sat down opposite the treasury, and watched the multitude putting money into the treasury. Many rich people put in large sums. And a poor widow came, and put in two copper coins, which make a penny. And he called his disciples to him, and said to them, "Truly, I say to you, this poor widow has put in more than all those who are contributing to the treasury. For they all contributed out of their abundance; but she out of her poverty has put in everything she had, her whole living."

Mark 12:41-44 RSV

How to Be Stewardly

So when you give to the needy, do not announce it with trumpets, as the hypocrites do in the synagogues and on the streets, to be honored by men. I tell you the truth, they have received their reward in full. But when you give to the needy, do not let your left hand know what your right hand is doing, so that your giving may be in secret.

Matthew 6:2-4

Command those who are rich in this present age not to be haughty, nor to trust in uncertain riches but in the living God, who gives us richly all things to enjoy. Let them do good, that they be rich in good works, ready to give, willing to share.

1 Timothy 6:17-18 NKJV

The Truth about Strength

The Lord is my strength and song, and he is become my salvation: he is my God, and I will prepare him an habitation; my father's God, and I will exalt him.

Exodus 15:2 KJV

He will give his people strength. He will bless them with peace.

Psalm 29:11 TLB

My grace is sufficient for you, for My strength is made perfect in weakness.

2 Corinthians 12:9 NKJV

Finally, my brethren, be strong in the Lord, and in the power of his might.

Ephesians 6:10 KJV

... He is my God, and I will praise him, my father's God, and I will exalt him.

Exodus 15:2

Make it your ambition to lead a quiet life, to mind your own business and to work with your hands, just as we told you, so that your daily life may win the respect of outsiders and so that you will not be dependent on anybody.

1 THESSALONIANS 4:11-12

"Be strong and courageous. Do not be afraid or terrified because of them, for the Lord your God goes with you; he will never leave you nor forsake you."

DEUTERONOMY 31:6

The name of the Lord is a strong tower; the righteous run to it and are safe.

PROVERBS 18:10

The Lord is with me; I will not be afraid. What can man do to me?

PSALM 118:6

He Is Strength

The Lord is my strength and my song; he has become my salvation.

Psalm 118:14

Behold, God is my salvation; I will trust, and will not be afraid; for the Lord God is my strength and my song, and he has become my salvation.

Isaiah 12:2 RSV

Sing aloud to God our strength; make a joyful shout to the God of Jacob.

Psalm 81:1 NKJV

My flesh and my heart fail; but God is the strength of my heart and my portion forever.

Psalm 73:26 NKJV

He Gives Strength

You armed me with strength for battle; you made my adversaries bow at my feet.

2 Samuel 22:40

It is God that girdeth me with strength, and maketh my way perfect.

Psalm 18:32 KJV

He giveth power to the faint; and to them that have no might he increaseth strength.

Isaiah 40:29 KJV

The Truth about Stress

You will keep in perfect peace him whose mind is steadfast, because he trusts in you. Trust in the Lord forever, for the Lord, the Lord, is the Rock eternal.

Isaiah 26:3-4

Come to Me, all you who labor and are heavy laden, and I will give you rest.

Matthew 11:28 NKJV

May the Lord of peace himself give you peace at all times and in every way.

2 Thessalonians 3:16

Moreover, when God gives any man wealth and possessions, and enables him to enjoy them, to accept his lot and be happy in his work – this is a gift of God.

Ecclesiastes 5:19

I urge you, brothers, by our Lord Jesus Christ and by the love of the Spirit, to join me in my struggle by praying to God for me.

ROMANS 15:30

"Your maxims are proverbs of ashes; your defenses are defenses of clay. Keep silent and let me speak; then let come to me what may."

JOB 13:12-13

Then Job replied: "I have heard many things like these; miserable comforters are you all! Will your long-winded speeches never end? What ails you that you keep on arguing?"

JOB 16:1-3

Consider him who endured such opposition from sinful men, so that you will not grow weary and lose heart.

HEBREWS 12:3

Finding Peace

I will listen to what God the Lord will say; he promises peace to his people, his saints.

Psalm 85:8

Great peace have they which love thy law: and nothing shall offend them.

Psalm 119:165 KJV

Therefore being justified by faith, we have peace with God through our Lord Jesus Christ.

Romans 5:1 KJV

And let the peace of God rule in your hearts, to the which also ye are called in one body; and be ye thankful.

Colossians 3:15 KJV

Godly Peace

Lord, You will establish peace for us, for You have also done all our works in us.

Isaiah 26:12 NKJV

Consider the blameless, observe the upright; there is a future for the man of peace.

Psalm 37:37

Those who trust in the Lord are like Mount Zion, which cannot be moved, but abides forever.

Psalm 125:1 NKJV

"And in this place I will grant peace," declares the Lord Almighty.

Haggai 2:9

And the peace of God, which passeth all understanding, shall keep your hearts and minds through Christ Jesus.

Philippians 4:7 KJV

The Truth about Success

True humility and respect for the Lord lead a man to riches, honor and long life.

PROVERBS 22:4 TLB

And, of course, it is very good if a man has received wealth from the Lord, and the good health to enjoy it. To enjoy your work and to accept your lot in life – that is indeed a gift from God.

ECCLESIASTES 5:19 TLB

You will decide on a matter, and it will be established for you, and light will shine on your ways.

JOB 22:28 RSV

Riches and honor are with me, enduring wealth and prosperity. My fruit is better than gold, even fine gold, and my yield than choice silver.

PROVERBS 8:18-19 RSV

"Be strong and very courageous. Be careful to obey all the law my servant Moses gave you; do not turn from it to the right or to the left, that you may be successful wherever you go."

Joshua 1:7

And the Lord was with him [Hezekiah]; he was successful in whatever he undertook. He rebelled against the king of Assyria and did not serve him.

2 Kings 18:7

"O Lord, let your ear be attentive to the prayer of this your servant and to the prayer of your servants who delight in revering your name. Give your servant success today by granting him favor ... "

Nehemiah 1:11

The Lord will protect him and preserve his life; he will bless him in the land and not surrender him to the desire of his foes.

Psalm 41:2

Heavenly Success

He should eat and drink and enjoy the fruits of his labors, for these are gifts from God.

Ecclesiastes 3:13 TLB

Wealth and riches are in his house, and his righteousness endures forever.

Psalm 112:3

Beloved, I pray that you may prosper in all things and be in health, just as your soul prospers.

3 John 2 NKJV

In My Father's house are many dwelling places; if it were not so, I would have told you; for I go to prepare a place for you. And if I go and prepare a place for you, I will come again, and receive you to Myself; that where I am, there you may be also.

John 14:2-3 NASB

Success on Earth

The Lord your God will make you abound in all the work of your hand, in the fruit of your body, in the increase of your livestock, and in the produce of your land for good.

Deuteronomy 30:9 NKJV

Blessed is every one who fears the Lord, who walks in His ways. When you eat the labor of your hands, you shall be happy, and it shall be well with you.

Psalm 128:1-2 NKJV

He shall be like a tree planted by the rivers of water, that brings forth its fruit in its season, whose leaf also shall not wither; and whatever he does shall prosper.

Psalm 1:3 NKJV

The Truth about Suffering

He is despised and rejected by men, a Man of sorrows and acquainted with grief. And we hid, as it were, our faces from Him; He was despised, and we did not esteem Him.

Isaiah 53:3 NKJV

He then began to teach them that the Son of Man must suffer many things and be rejected by the elders, chief priests and teachers of the law, and that he must be killed and after three days rise again.

Mark 8:31

"Yet man is born to trouble as surely as sparks fly upward."

Job 5:7

For our light and momentary troubles are achieving for us an eternal glory that far outweighs them all.

2 Corinthians 4:17

My God, my God, why have you forsaken me? Why are you so far from saving me, so far from the words of my groaning? O my God, I cry out by day, but you do not answer, by night, and am not silent.

PSALM 22:1-2

Perseverance must finish its work so that you may be mature and complete, not lacking anything.

JAMES 1:4

For when we came into Macedonia, this body of ours had no rest, but we were harassed at every turn – conflicts on the outside, fears within.

2 CORINTHIANS 7:5

I know, O Lord, that your laws are righteous, and in faithfulness you have afflicted me.

PSALM 119:75

How to Handle Suffering

That is why, for Christ's sake, I delight in weaknesses, in insults, in hardships, in persecutions, in difficulties. For when I am weak, then I am strong.

2 Corinthians 12:10

For I consider that the sufferings of this present time are not worthy to be compared with the glory which shall be revealed in us.

Romans 8:18 NKJV

Thou therefore endure hardness, as a good soldier of Jesus Christ.

2 Timothy 2:3 KJV

For to you it has been granted on behalf of Christ, not only to believe in Him, but also to suffer for His sake.

Philippians 1:29 NKJV

Triumph over Suffering

A righteous man may have many troubles, but the Lord delivers him from them all.

Psalm 34:19

Blessed is the man who endures temptation; for when he has been proved, he will receive the crown of life which the Lord has promised to those who love Him.

James 1:12 NKJV

Because he himself suffered when he was tempted, he is able to help those who are being tempted.

Hebrews 2:18

Share with me in the sufferings for the gospel according to the power of God, who has saved us and called us with a holy calling, not according to our works, but according to His own purpose and grace which was given to us in Christ Jesus ...

2 Timothy 1:8-9 NKJV

The Truth about Temptation

Put on the whole armor of God, that you may be able to stand against the wiles of the devil.

Ephesians 6:11 NKJV

Be self-controlled and alert. Your enemy the devil prowls around like a roaring lion looking for someone to devour.

1 Peter 5:8

For our light and momentary troubles are achieving for us an eternal glory that far outweighs them all.

2 Corinthians 4:17

The Lord knows how to deliver the godly out of temptations and to reserve the unjust under punishment for the day of judgment.

2 Peter 2:9 NKJV

Watch and pray so that you will not fall into temptation. The spirit is willing, but the body is weak.

MARK 14:38

Therefore, since we are surrounded by such a great cloud of witnesses, let us throw off everything that hinders and the sin that so easily entangles, and let us run with perseverance the race marked out for us.

HEBREWS 12:1

Watch your life and doctrine closely. Persevere in them, because if you do, you will save both yourself and your hearers.

1 TIMOTHY 4:16

Because he himself suffered when he was tempted, he is able to help those who are being tempted.

HEBREWS 2:18

HELP FROM GOD

No temptation has overtaken you that is not common to man. God is faithful, and he will not let you be tempted beyond your strength, but with the temptation will also provide the way of escape, that you may be able to endure it.

1 CORINTHIANS 10:13 RSV

For since he himself has now been through suffering and temptation, he knows what it is like when we suffer and are tempted, and he is wonderfully able to help us.

HEBREWS 2:18 TLB

You are of God, little children, and have overcome them, because He who is in you is greater than he who is in the world.

1 JOHN 4:4 NKJV

Tempting Others

Therefore let us not judge one another anymore, but rather resolve this, not to put a stumbling block or a cause to fall in our brother's way.

Romans 14:13 NKJV

Do not cause anyone to stumble, whether Jews, Greeks or the church of God.

1 Corinthians 10:32

Let us therefore be diligent to enter that rest, lest anyone fall according to the same example of disobedience.

Hebrews 4:11 NKJV

The Truth about Thankfulness

Let your roots grow down into him and draw up nourishment from him. See that you go on growing in the Lord, and become strong and vigorous in the truth you were taught. Let your lives overflow with joy and thanksgiving for all he has done.

Colossians 2:7 TLB

And whatever you do or say, let it be as a representative of the Lord Jesus, and come with him into the presence of God the Father to give him your thanks.

Colossians 3:17 TLB

Sing to the Lord with thanksgiving; make music to our God on the harp.

Psalm 147:7

I thank my God every time I remember you.

Philippians 1:3

Let the word of Christ dwell in you richly as you teach and admonish one another with all wisdom, and as you sing psalms, hymns and spiritual songs with gratitude in your hearts to God.

COLOSSIANS 3:16

Cast your bread upon the waters, for after many days you will find it again. Give portions to seven, yes to eight, for you do not know what disaster may come upon the land.

ECCLESIASTES 11:1-2

This service that you perform is not only supplying the needs of God's people but is also overflowing in many expressions of thanks to God.

2 CORINTHIANS 9:12

Therefore, since we are receiving a kingdom that cannot be shaken, let us be thankful, and so worship God acceptably with reverence and awe, for our "God is consuming fire."

HEBREWS 12:28-29

Giving Thanks

Thanks be to God, who gives us the victory through our Lord Jesus Christ.

1 Corinthians 15:57 NASB

But thanks be to God, who always leads us in triumphal procession in Christ and through us spreads everywhere the fragrance of the knowledge of him.

2 Corinthians 2:14

In everything give thanks; for this is the will of God in Christ Jesus for you.

1 Thessalonians 5:18 NKJV

Songs of Thanksgiving

Give thanks to the Lord, for he is good; his love endures forever. Let them give thanks to the Lord for his unfailing love and his wonderful deeds for men.

Psalm 107:1, 21

Then he turned my sorrow into joy! He took away my clothes of mourning and gave me gay and festive garments to rejoice in so that I might sing glad praises to the Lord ... O Lord my God, I will keep on thanking you forever!

Psalm 30:11-12 TLB

O come, let us sing for joy to the Lord; let us shout joyfully to the rock of our salvation. Let us come before His presence with thanksgiving; let us shout joyfully to Him with psalms.

Psalm 95:1-2 NASB

The Truth about Tragedy

Even when walking through the dark valley of death I will not be afraid, for you are close beside me, guarding, guiding all the way.

Psalm 23:4 TLB

Weeping may remain for a night, but rejoicing comes in the morning.

Psalm 30:5

"He will wipe every tear from their eyes. There will be no more death or mourning or crying or pain, for the old order of things has passed away." He who was seated on the throne said, "I am making everything new!" Then he said, "Write this down, for these words are trustworthy and true."

Revelation 21:4-5

When you pass through the waters, I will be with you; and through the rivers, they shall not overflow you. When you walk through the fire, you shall not be burned, nor shall the flame scorch you.

ISAIAH 43:2 NKJV

I will not leave you as orphans; I will come to you.

JOHN 14:18

The hearts of the people cry out to the Lord. O wall of the Daughter of Zion, let your tears flow like a river day and night; give yourself no relief, your eyes no rest.

LAMENTATIONS 2:18

The Lord has heard my cry for mercy; the Lord accepts my prayer.

PSALM 6:9

"What I feared has come upon me; what I dreaded has happened to me. I have no peace, no quietness; I have no rest, but only turmoil."

JOB 3:25-26

Dealing with Tragedy

He gives power to the tired and worn out, and strength to the weak.
Isaiah 40:29 TLB

Those who mourn are fortunate! for they shall be comforted.
Matthew 5:4 TLB

Come to Me, all who are weary and heavy-laden, and I will give you rest.
Matthew 11:28 NASB

Let not your heart be troubled; you believe in God, believe also in Me.
John 14:1 NKJV

God's Presence in Tragedy

God sets the lonely in families, he leads forth the prisoners with singing.

Psalm 68:6

He heals the brokenhearted and binds up their wounds.

Psalm 147:3 NKJV

Arise, shine; for your light has come, and the glory of the Lord has risen upon you. For behold, darkness will cover the earth, and deep darkness the peoples; but the Lord will rise upon you, and His glory will appear upon you.

Isaiah 60:1-2 NASB

For Thou hast been a defense for the helpless, a defense for the needy in his distress, a refuge from the storm, a shade from the heat.

Isaiah 25:4 NASB

The Truth about Unemployment

The Lord himself goes before you and will be with you; he will never leave you nor forsake you. Do not be afraid; do not be discouraged.

DEUTERONOMY 31:8

Thus says the Lord, your Redeemer, the Holy One of Israel: "I am the Lord your God, Who teaches you to profit, Who leads you by the way you should go."

ISAIAH 48:17 NKJV

Dear brothers, is your life full of difficulties and temptations? Then be happy, for when the way is rough, your patience has a chance to grow. So let it grow, and don't try to squirm out of your problems. For when your patience is finally in full bloom, then you will be ready for anything, strong in character, full and complete.

JAMES 1:2-4 TLB

When You Face Unemployment

Fear of man is a dangerous trap, but to trust in God means safety.

Proverbs 29:25 TLB

Blessed is the man who trusts in the Lord and whose trust is the Lord. For he will be like a tree planted by the water, that extends its roots by a stream and will not fear when the heat comes; but its leaves will be green, and it will not be anxious in a year of drought nor cease to yield fruit.

Jeremiah 17:7-8 NASB

And God is able to make all grace abound to you, that always having all sufficiency in everything, you may have an abundance for every good deed.

2 Corinthians 9:8 NASB

God's Presence

And your ears will hear a word behind you, "This is the way, walk in it," whenever you turn to the right or to the left.

Isaiah 30:21 NASB

Remember, your Father knows exactly what you need even before you ask him!

Matthew 6:8 TLB

Hope does not disappoint us, because God has poured out his love into our hearts by the Holy Spirit, whom he has given us.

Romans 5:5

The Truth about Wisdom

If you want to know what God wants you to do, ask him, and he will gladly tell you, for he is always ready to give a bountiful supply of wisdom to all who ask him; he will not resent it.

James 1:5 TLB

Praise be to the name of God for ever and ever; wisdom and power are his. He reveals deep and hidden things; he knows what lies in darkness, and light dwells with him.

Daniel 2:20, 22

In whom are hid all the treasures of wisdom and knowledge.

Colossians 2:3 KJV

God's Wisdom

I will praise the Lord, who counsels me; even at night my heart instructs me.

Psalm 16:7

Yes, if you want better insight and discernment, and are searching for them as you would for lost money or hidden treasure, then wisdom will be given you, and knowledge of God himself; you will soon learn the importance of reverence for the Lord and of trusting him. For the Lord grants wisdom! His every word is a treasure of knowledge and understanding.

Proverbs 2:3-7 TLB

The Lord by wisdom founded the earth; by understanding He established the heavens.

Proverbs 3:19 NKJV

Man's Wisdom

For the foolishness of God is wiser than men, and the weakness of God is stronger than men.

1 Corinthians 1:25 RSV

For since in the wisdom of God the world through its wisdom did not come to know God, God was well-pleased through the foolishness of the message preached to save those who believe.

1 Corinthians 1:21 NASB

Because the foolishness of God is wiser than men, and the weakness of God is stronger than men. For consider your calling, brethren, that there were not many wise according to the flesh, not many mighty, not many noble; but God has chosen the foolish things of the world to shame the wise, and God has chosen the weak things of the world to shame the things which are strong.

1 Corinthians 1:25-27 NASB